American Gods

Míra Vísté

Cadmus Publishing
www.cadmuspublishing.com

Copyright © Míra Vísté

Cover art by Francisco Moraga – fjmoragaproductions@gmail.com

Published by Cadmus Publishing
www.cadmuspublishing.com
Port Angeles, WA

ISBN: 978-1-63751-246-3

All rights reserved. Copyright under Berne Copyright Convention, Universal Copyright Convention, and Pan-American Copyright Convention. No part of this book may be reproduced, stored in a retrieval system, or transmitted in any form, or by any means, electronic, mechanical, photocopying, recording or otherwise, without prior permission of the author.

Acknowledgements

Goddess by Vaneese: song: MyVsky Mayovsky A perfect most beautiful reflection of My Goddess Mighty ISHTAR whom all the Gods have bowed down to. The Goddess of Love and War and mistress to all the living Gods. You are the brightest light in Seattle, Washington and I truly bow down to your beauty.

The phone call by Ramirez/Latino Heat Album. It was my old school homies and Players in the game when I was growing up that taught me and showed me that their will always be somebody bigger than you. Mark these truths or else the cloak of lies blind you forever. Gardens of the Moon by Steven Erickson (book). This book is from my House to yours with nothing but Love & Respect for this current life. Not the next one or the one before but this 1. We got movies, raps and books for you to see what were talking about. I'm expecting every song, book and movie to be watched listened to and read so you can coralate it with your real life. Its 2023 What teams were in the NBA finals? Record breaking heat in Seattle. What is the name of the album by Ramirez I just mentioned. Servin Heat by South Central Cartel. Look up mind control in a Websters dictionary? Why is it not in there? We all know what it means. Show some respect to the players in the game. U.S.A. love. Lets ride Independent and create something that will last into the future. Some of you hav been under the boat so long you like it. Gardens of the Moon.

TABLE OF CONTENTS

Chapter 1 1
Chapter 2 8
Chapter 3 19
Chapter 4 28
Chapter 5 36
Chapter 6 43
Chapter 7 52
Chapter 8 60
Chapter 9 64

Chapter 1

First, let me thank you for your time as it is my intention to make it worth your precious time. Also, let us thank and acknowledge the greatest nation, the United States of America, for these opportunities. Learning the truth and striving for knowledge and a better life for all, especially oneself. To be happy and satisfied should be everyone's goal and right. Now, let us truly try to see things for what they are and not as how we see things ourselves.

To do this, we must detach ourselves from all influences, feelings, and all that we know to be our reality. We must question everything we know. We must understand what our constitution means when it says that we are all created equal. Take it all away and we only have our minds. It is the most powerful weapon we have. The founding fathers knew and understood this, and it must be fought for.

For the sake of argument, let us agree that when we are born, none of us would be able to survive without help. We have been taught everything we know, and the truth is unless you question everything and seek the truth for yourself, we are irrelevant. So let us move forward in truth and honesty for all of our sakes. Now, let's agree that we do not know everything and maybe no one does, including our ancestral alien God's.

Let us say you believe in Christianity's God, and he knows everything. He punished men for eating the fruit of knowledge and the truth is he did not bestow his knowledge to us and teach us everything or we would be in a totally different place right now. Let's keep it real, there are a bunch of idiots leading a bunch of idiots and it shows.

Why would you take advice from artists, actors, or politicians that would say and do anything for power and money? Why was Trump the best president we have ever had regardless of his big mouth? He does not have to like me, he just has to like our country, as we all should. We've all been through some shit and go through it sometimes.

I'm from California until I moved to Washington state. If you run a make on me, you will see that I have a criminal record and if you a player in the game, I'm 10 feet deep in this shit and got the game to prove it. Most people cannot even fathom this shit and if you never stop and look and listen, you will never know it.

My house put this movie out for me when a rival put a hit on me and sent a crooked cop to do it. A cop literally intercepted my phone so I couldn't call out then came into my house claiming I was overdosing. He tried to inject me with a needle until some girl called me knowing that the cop was trying to kill me. She saved me and my family's life by staying on the phone with me as I gave her his name. I told her how they tried to slip me a mickey earlier that day. The police officer left, saying he would be back, but he never came. That was my awakening into the life.

The movie is called Dirty and that is what it's about, but to people that don't know what's up, it is just a movie but for us in the know, it's all game. It is representing and talking real shit. If you look at the bonus footage, the artist taboo lets you know he plays my character. If you have ever seen that movie before, it was just a movie but now that you know more about it, you'll see it differently. You have to know what to look for.

Now, imagine all the shit we are missing because we don't know what to look for. That is why we should always question everything around us so that people don't run game on you without you knowing. All this shit is done right under your noses. If we are doing that, imagine what the government is doing. You think the government would not do that, but have you seen the movie Sicario? That is our shit too and we are saying something. Everything has a meaning.

We have got music out and they talk about this shit, now this might be too much for your chicken shit feelings but it's true. It is a crooked ass world we live in, my friend, and it is a fact that the government is involved. I have had police officers cover up crimes for me. There are some powerful people out there and it is not a game. We are talking about companies, banks, hospitals, cops and government and they are all in on this shit. All with the business and we are not playing out here. You have to take care of business. The reasons are very clear why this is so important. Read the book: Tranceformation of America by Cathy OBrien & Mark Phillips It clearly talks about these tactics being used on everyday Americans. Its the programming of our minds. If you can truly get what Im saying you'll start to understand why we must question everything.

Check this song out by a solid ass rapper. He made it when I was fighting a rival over some turf issues sleeper cell by conejo. I was going to college for a business degree and even that was somebody's turf. They were pushing girls out of there and what not but my Microsoft class man, they were all up in the computer, talking to me as I tried to do my assignments. They were harassing me, talking shit. Then I had someone named Peter who was an Arab calling me on a number from Washington D.C and he would tip me off on shit like he was listening to all my conversations and knew everything that was going on.

There was also spyware on my phone. All they seemed to need was my email address and they had total access to my phone. Nothing was sacred and they track you like that. I said I was intrigued by technology because all this tech and power. So, if we know that everyone is looking and listening, then we have to use this to our advantage. Listen to the song called Sleeper Cell by Conejo and you'll notice when he says what if those powers that be, be the same ones that took down the 3 towers.

We know that on 9/11, 2 planes hit but three towers fell. By the way, I tried to join the marines the day after 9/11 but they said no because I only had a G.E.D. I tried to serve three times. Now, the patriot act is used on us. The boat I worked on in Alaska was called the "Alaska Patriot" and you can consider this book an act of patriotism and we are the ones they are using it on.

I truly do not care if you like it or not. This is reality. They never found the black boxes from the planes, which has never happened before plus three towers fell but only two buildings were hit. Let's keep it real, those are facts, we did not make that shit up. It is a crooked ass world and if you think the government wouldn't do that to us, look at what the Democrats did to Trump. Look how the SBA & DOJ tried to label parents as domestic terrorists. What happened during hurricane Katrina when they managed to take the guns from law abiding citizens so they could not even defend themselves. The truth is, they do not give a fuck about us. Look how the police officers arrested the father and daughter during the pandemic for playing in the park. Do you see any humanity in that?

A cop wanted to beat my ass one time for smoking on the sidewalk. I mean, shit, we cannot even breathe out here. I was 15 years old when I first got my ass kicked by the cops in Sacramento, California. Shit, while they were tossing us and beating us, the girls we were with were crying and I told one of them to call the cops because I thought these cops were going to kill us. You know, I thought I was tough at 15 and those cops had me cuffed up, face down with their knee on the back of my neck and asked me who the driver was. They yanked my hands up my back until I screamed is name in pain. This made me feel like a pussy, but my homie told me it was alright, they do this shit all the time.

Do you know why they beat our asses? They beat our asses because we parked in the wrong parking spot. Police brutality is very real, and they do not just kill black people. BLM is dumb as fuck. The police will kill anyone. I hate them because they kill innocent people, and nothing happens to them. We need accountability and that is a fact. Shit, I did 70 months in prison for an argument where no one was injured.

I pulled out a work box cutter on my girl at the time. Ironically, I pulled it out to make her sit down so we did not get pulled over by a cop. It worked. She sat down in the car as we were on the freeway. She was in the passenger seat. I mean, if I had really wanted to, I could have used it on her easily at any point, but it was clearly not my intention as I dropped her off at her mom's house. I apologized in the car before I dropped her off because she got scared.

I called later, laughing because I thought it was cute, she got scared when she shouldve known I would never hurt her. I had real things to worry about plus I have had D.V.'s in the past and violence is never the right answer in any relationship. I was young and stupid when I caught my D.V (domestic violence). For that argument, I was charged with second degree assault of the mental, second-degree kidnapping because she was in my car, and two unlawful imprisonments because her kids were in the back seat and then harassment because I called to apologize to her as well as to see if we were going to meet up that weekend.

It was the stupidest shit in my life, and I got 70 months for it. That is what is wrong with the justice system and how it is systematically racists towards minorities. So many people are incarcerated over exaggerated crimes. I was an iron worker for the union, and I was doing good. Do you know how many jobs I have lost over stupid arrests? I got pulled over for studded tires which I have because it snows where I live, but I forgot to change them for the summer, so I got pulled over. It was my work car and I commuted in this car and sometimes slept in it when I traveled, so my garbage was in the back seat.

There were empty beer cans in the car and for some fucking reason, that is illegal even though no one was drinking, so I got taken to jail. I lost my job and then got hit with a ticket. How was I supposed to pay for that shit? This shit does not make sense. I am locked up right now on a double murder of my Uncle's with nothing but weak and at best circumstantial evidence. There were not any witnesses or murder weapons or a motive, but a witness two blocks away that could not even point me out in two-line ups. Spokane is the most policed city I have ever seen, and they discriminate against their population, I am proof of that. I mean, the jury was falling asleep at my trial.

Obviously, I did not do this shit, but I need an act of the Goddess to help me right now. Luminata Law took my case and even had Professor Loftus from University of Washington who wrote a professional essay in my favor and the state is trying to fight to discredit it. Denied my appeal. How can a case based on pure circumstantial evidence not have issues.

Chapter 2

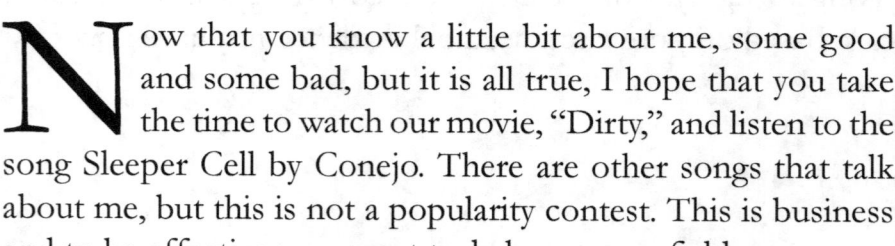

Now that you know a little bit about me, some good and some bad, but it is all true, I hope that you take the time to watch our movie, "Dirty," and listen to the song Sleeper Cell by Conejo. There are other songs that talk about me, but this is not a popularity contest. This is business and to be effective, you must truly know your field.

I know this lifestyle from a player's perspective and everything that is involved. You cannot trust anyone, and this game is so fucking cold that some piece of shits out there will kill your wife and kids, family, and girl. Like, their crazy or something. I mean, this shit gets so fucking intense that the little things can mean so much. An act of kindness from a complete stranger would just touch my soul.

So, naturally, if they are getting at you in really crazy ways, you have to get crazy also. I do not and never have hurt innocent women and children, but I will definitely serve someone who does. So, staying true to ourselves, we have to question everything. Why is it like this? Everybody that I have worked with, whether it was in Alaska, in the Union, telemarketing or as a janitor, every time people were using some kind of drug. Shit, I have seen Pastor's doing drugs. I mean, look at Hunter Biden. This shit is everywhere, so why don't they just legalize drugs?

These are significant issues that are important to our society. If the government regulated drugs like they do with Marijuana, imagine how many fewer overdoses there would be. It would be so beneficial to the community. There would be less crime, some piece of mind, and there would be happiness in our lives. Why don't they?

I mean, look at these idiots in leadership like Nancy Pelosi and all of the other weird people that really have no business being in congress trying to pass their woke agenda. I mean, look at the shit we are dealing with out here. First, they should let us be human out here, but they are as fake as the artists, actors, and the media on television. We need people like Tulsi Gabbard as president. She would be the perfect divinely beautiful woman president. We need to oust the losers and vote in some True Americans. Independant Party.

We are all in this together because we are all human and we all have minds to use as our greatest weapon. So, let us use this opportunity to unite and create something together to help evolve our society. Okay, so you can see right now, I am going on about what I am saying in this book but everywhere you look, people are going on about some shit. How grounded and real are they with that shit?

Let's take climate change seriously for a minute. We know climate change is a real thing as there is proof of an Ice Age and a great flood. We have cities that are underwater from ancient civilizations, and we find seashells on the mountains, which proves that those mountains were underwater at some point in our history. It is a fact that earth changes and the ancient alien Gods and Goddesses could not stop it from happening. So, what makes you think that regulating emissions will?

To stop something like global warming, you would have to control the weather. So, it seems to me that politicians are approaching climate change with ulterior motives because you would think that if they genuinely cared about us, they would be creating a path for Americans to survive such a change. Okay, so when a hurricane hits, we can prepare for it by boarding up windows and leaving town. So, why are we not truly preparing for climate change?

How is climate change going to affect our geographical area? Instead, we are on some transgender bullshit. So, climate change must not be real, or our government does not give a shit about us. Remember 9/11 and Trump? JFKJ. That was the government. The same assholes in there right now, including Nancy Pelosi and Joe Biden, getting rich off politics. They are the same idiots who are pushing climate change.

Let's check these people out because other than Donald Trump, both democrats and republicans are about a New World Order. What does that even mean and how is it even possible? You know, I cannot even leave this country because I am a felon. If there is a New World Order, that means that our constitution no longer exists to us. So, what would our rights be and who will lead the world, and for what reasons? I mean, why would we want these losers in congress who cannot even keep it real with their constituents, leading the world?

We would definitely have to follow the science, but as you can see with the pandemic, you cannot trust the Doctors and the politicians to follow the science. If that is the case, we cannot give up our constitutional rights to these people that do not care about us. It is a fact that the media is working with the government, so you cannot trust them because they are pushing a biased agenda.

They lied to us and that is the ultimate betrayal in their field. The democrats were trying to pass house bills without allowing us to know about them or what was in those bills and that is a betrayal to all of us in their field. That means that the media and the politicians do not care about us, and these are facts. They want to take our guns, but why don't they take the cops guns first? We see how police officers will kill anyone and how they will arrest you without any humanity.

We should never give our weapons up as that is the only protection that we have from them. When that police officer came to kill me, he asked me if I had any guns in the house and I told him no. Then he reached for a syringe to give me a hot shot. He only had a gun on his ankle and was in an unmarked car. I could not even use the phone to call out because he scrambled it.

That was in 2005, just four years after September 11th. Now, we just had a pandemic, and you see what the government did with its emergency powers that they invoked. Now, they do not want to lift those emergency powers. These politicians are the real dictators who are trying to stay in power. It is a fact and not all politicians are like that, but this is what the new world order is supposed to look like.

President Donald Trump is a American who loves this country and that is why people like him. Who cares if you do not like him? We cannot be forced to like someone. Fuck Trump, but he was the best president in our lifetime and the government hated on him just like they hate on us. Even the Churches are corrupted by the government. Why do you think that Arab that would call me and say that his name was Peter ended up doing that? Reffering to the song Sleeper Cell by Conejo.

After the cop tried to kill me, I went to Church and filled out a prayer request form and the Pastor told me how Jesus asked Peter three times if he loved him. Then he told me that there was a bunch of scientists involved and that the mind is an enormously powerful thing. They fabricated a prayer book for me called, "The Upper Room," and it was talking shit to me because I beat up a marine.

The Church said that it was called staying above the snake line. CNN ran the story word for word about what I put on that prayer request form. I could not even go to church. Look at George Floyd rests in peace and so many more victims of police killings but what you have with Mr. Floyd was the weaponized version. The county coroner and all of them were protecting each other. They had to bring someone from outside the city to bring the truth out.

That is what I am going through right now, as my trial was in Spokane and my appeal was in Spokane as well. I have been asking for a change of venue for that reason. When you live in a city your dealing with the city government.

Now, let's get into another betrayal of government. Why do we not have the right to defend ourselves? Kyle Rittenhouse was a win but only because it was on the news and even then, the democrats were against him. It seems like democrats are what is wrong with our society. I knew a guy in jail that had been arrested because someone shot his car. People getting arrested for shooting someone who is robbing their house. Why can't we protect ourselves? In this new world order, we cannot protect our property and family because it is not ours, that is the only reason of which I can think. So, if it is not ours than who's is it?

Now, lets talk about taxes and why we are getting taxed just to be treated this way. Is that the new world order? I have had many jobs and paid my taxes. I was a fisherman in Alaska on a long liner for three years, working sixteen-hour days, seven days a week and one time I made $24,000. After taxes, they left me with $11,000. I paid $8,000 on social security alone and at the end of the year, I still owed $300.

I get harassed by the police officers and the government everywhere that I go, and I cannot smoke in public, and I can't defend myself plus I can't leave the country. I cannot find a place to rent because I am a felon, so I have to live in the ghetto where my mailbox was getting broken into every day. I could hear my neighbor snoring and I was paying $650 for a one-bedroom apartment plus I could not go to college or to church. This is in Washington State and now, I am in prison which apparently is the only place I can go, and they are still taking 45% of all my money that is sent in.

This state is run by democrats, and this is the systematic racism and exactly why we should not be talking about a new world order. I hate being locked up with a passion, so much so that when I got out in 2014 after doing 7 years for an argument, I said I would never come back so I was going to college, and I was being harassed through Microsoft Word technology.

I have never been married and I do not have kids for these reasons. I trust no one and always slept with a weapon when I was out of prison. Have you ever seen the movie, "Enemy of the State," with Will Smith? These politicians do not deserve to have that power because they do not care about us.

Now, let's talk about these companies and why they are democrats. It makes sense that these people would be democrats because they operate on a global scale. We know that companies do not give a shit about us either. If it was not for the unions, they would support child labor. They are in it for the money and power just like politicians. Republicans do not care about us either or they would be doing something about this.

I am not political but when we lost our smoking rights, we lost our freedom in principle. Shouldn't it be up to store owners whether they allow smoking in their establishment or not? If someone does not want to be around it, they could go somewhere else, shit. They only go on about it for the money. What do they do with the money? Miss me with that shit, "my grandparents both died of cancer." If you really care, donate, and raise money for St. Jude or something. Do not tell me what I should do, that is none of anyone's business.

You see how far these losers went during the pandemic, trying to tell us who we can have over for the holidays. How Michelle Obama tried to tell us what to eat. Fauci should be fired. They are not fit to lead, just like the woke movement has no business in schools or in the military. The woke and special interest are going on about stupid shit that has nothing to do with education. Naturaly people want attention. They'll do anything for it.

So, we know our minds are a powerful thing, but everything that we are being taught is manmade, including Christianity. Read, "Astral Worship," by J.H. Hill. It is a noticeably short but powerful non-fiction book on how Christianity was made. We should be taught the unbiased truth so we can learn from it. Our American, Mexican, White, Black, Asian, and French histories. The most crucial time for our brains to develop is kindergarten through 12th grades and that is where we should start introducing all of the fundamental break throughs in Math, Science, History and mental developments. The superhuman capabilities that our minds are capable of should be taught as well as technology.

Another question I have is why wouldn't we make it mandatory for everyone ages 18 to 20 to serve in the military and learn the basics of survival and discipline, patriotism, and respect for our country? Learn all the combat skills to defend ourselves and our country. Create unity. The truth is that our leaders are creating problems as they are unfit to lead. If we are to survive anything that we go through, we must be prepared.

I am sure that our military is very capable, but we must be treated equally if not greater than our police. We all serve our country. Companies should be doing the same. We all should be benefiting our society and serving our country. Where do these people get off with the one world order stuff? The only way you can have that is if the world united and agreed as one, but you have so many different countries and beliefs. We should be one nation united which would insure our futures. You might think that your life is different from mine, but in the end, we are all human and humans are stupid and imperfect.

People are always going on about something like it is new or has never been done before. The truth is that we are new. Our country is new. Have you ever read the history of the Anunnaki? So, it is said that they created us through their DNA with genetic manipulation, but Enlil was disgusted by the humans because they were loud, multiplied like crazy, were gay, and would mate with animals. That was written way before our time.

Gay people have the same rights now and that should be enough. Let's keep it real, a man has a penis, and a woman has a vagina. If you do not like what you were born with and want to be transgender, then that is a personal mental problem and your own choice. However, denying our true genders makes you irrelevant for a serious conversation. That is denying reality and the truth is key for all progress and success for our future.

The truth is that it should not matter what your sexual preferences are. That is between you and your lovers. If you have a dick, use the men's bathroom. If you have a pussy, use the woman's bathroom. We all have to piss and shit out of what we are born with. So, you have it bad because you are gay, black, white, Mexican, or Asian but that is the way that it is until we can stand together as a united front and make an effort to change our society.

Check this out, we know a lot of this shit is all mental and proper preparation prevents poor performance. Nine times out of ten, you can win or lose a fight before it even starts. Let's keep it real, most of these people are faking the funk. Like all the BLM protesters instigating shit. If you run their bitch asses over, they will cry about it, yet they are ruining neighborhoods and harassing people. Shit, get in my face while I am eating. I would bang it out with them. I wish I could be there. I would sit down with my white folks eating with them with my gun on me and if BLM wants to disrespect me, I would bang it out with those clowns and make sure they never do it again.

I hate bullies. You know, you might think that I am crazy or that I am violent but there is a right and a wrong way on how to do things. Leave innocent women and children out of shit. Look at how they are acting, like it is all about black people. Come to the hood and act stupid like that and I would shoot you to.

We should be writing some legislature for police accountability. Cops have killed so many innocent people. I remember when the news showed the police officers beating a white guy to death. He was yelling for his father and saying that they were killing him while the cops beat him to death. Those are bitch ass police officers for you and what they are known for. Remember how the Amber alert law came to be? Do you remember how they changed the law because of her? It took one victim to change it so why can't we have police accountability across the board for George Floyd and all of the innocent victims of police brutality?

We get nothing for our money. We must be color blind in our society and look past our identities to advance our human race and lead our country into the future. You know, I was always getting picked on my whole life. I had a high-pitched voice so I sounded like a girl and other people would make fun of me for that shit. I was always getting picked on by older fools. At the arcade, motherfuckers would steal my quarters and push me out of the way to play my game. I would go to the store, and somebody would try to take my candy money. Do you know what I mean?

Every time something would happen, my brother, family, or homies would stand up for me because it was the right thing to do. I did not even know I was Mexican until I got into Junior High School and that was because Mexicans were beefing with the Asians in my school. When I was still growing up, I wanted to be a skateboarder like Tony Hawk and Christian

Okoy. Santa Cruz, California is the most beautiful place that I have every lived. Skateboarding and surfing was the lifestyle. Situation Critical by Andre Nictiatina: song

Chapter 3

If you have read that book, "Astral Worship," and recognize that the human race is not perfect, then we can also agree that our minds are a powerful thing, meaning we should then be perfectly capable of achieving anything and everything. Everything around us is man-made. So, we know man is not perfect, therefore, we should not let a human tell us what to believe but rather we should rely on truth.

Alien's, God's, and Science. Christianity itself is a man-made religion and that's a fact. Christianity is good in principle for a civilization, but it is unrealistic and falls short as it is based on lies. They are trying to create a perfect man but their idea of perfect man is ridiculous and unachievable. It is fake and they used to kill you if you believed otherwise, so why would you believe in something that was forced on our ancestors?

When that cop came to kill me, I called out for God, but God will not save you and no, you are not meant to suffer. All that is caused by man. It is almost like the founding fathers knew this when they made the constitution. We have a right to pursue happiness. In the Churches prime, what happened? The inquisition. They took shit way too far and that is what our government is doing to us. Regulating companies, creating laws, taxing us, and policing us to death.

If we have a taillight out, they arrest us and give us a ticket. A politician embezzles our money and spends it on special interests that make them rich like climate change and nothing happens to them. Who are they? Are politicians not elected by the people? How many times do they promise to do shit and then when they get elected, they betray us and start talking about the new world order?

Look at Joe Biden, George Bush Senior and his son, and Obama. Politics should be left out of congress and any other public institution like schools and police and government. It should have no influence on our country's future and progress. Things like pro-life and choice issues should be simple. If you want an abortion, you should pay for it. It is your body and your bed so you have to sleep in it. Let us say that you can't afford it, well that is why we should tell the government to quit taking all of our money, so that you can afford it. Accidents do happen, but if I break my cup on accident, should you pay for it? If anything, insurance should cover abortions.

The same can be said of fossil fuels. Why should we pay more for gas food when all we have to do is supply our own? Just because you want green technology does not mean that you should be able to handicap us. The politicians still use fossil fuels so why can't we? We work for everything we have so why can't we have both?

I do not know what it would take for these career politicians to realize that they are not fit to lead. They think they are better than us and even want to tell us how to live. Instead, they should tell us the truth and let us decide. A politician that thinks that they are better than us should automatically get impeached as unfit for duty. Anyone trying to change our constitutional rights should automatically get impeached for treason against our country. We should buy an island with our tax money and send these people and politicians that believe in anything other than our constitution to that Island so that they can govern themselves and see how they are unfit to lead.

We do not need human dictators to tell us what to do when we have Goddesses, Gods, science, math, truth, country, and a mind to do it. We should test every politician before they take their oath in office. A test of logic and all kinds of unbiased questions and scenarios. This will show if they are truly fit to lead, and need to prove their loyalty. We earn shit around here so they should to. Who should be number 1 here? Americans should be number 1.

The movies, "Sicario," part 1 and part 2, the movie "Dirty," are both movies that are based on some truths. The music Sleeper Cell by Conejo, Meet Me in the Sky by Bone thugs N' Harmony, He not Siciliano by conejo and Cause it's real by Conejo are about me and what I was going through at the time. I mean it when I say that we are all in this together. Trust nobody. You have companies selling our information. Everyone I knew covered their cameras on their laptops with tape because the government or anyone can spy on you. All they needed was an e-mail address and they had total control over my phone. This was in 2014, so you can imagine how bad it will get.

If we know that our minds are our most powerful thing, it is only natural that people in power would want to keep you from knowing the truth. Now, they are in your kids' schools, teaching them man-made philosophies and opinions like a dictatorship. When I went to school, I grew up pledging allegiance to the flag in school. That is a good thing, as it creates unity. If you are offended, then get the fuck out of this country. You have no business complaining about this country's patriotism. This is our home. It is not Mexico, China, Africa, Europe, or the Middle East.

We are all here for a reason because this country was made to be better. The Civil War happened, and we won. Martin Luther King Jr. had his dream, and it came true. Women got their voting rights and gay people can marry now. No one has ever just given me something and we work hard for our shit. We are all just trying to have something, but it feels like politicans just want to take it from us.

Now, lets talk about our American history for a bit. The Native Americans are native to North and Central America. The Europeans, French, Spaniards and Portuguese invaded these lands for the gold and the land. They did it in the name of their man-made religion. The terror they caused on the Natives can still be seen by the number of Catholics and Christians in this area. Black and White people are foreigners here so if they do not like it, why don't they go back to their native lands? I am sure they are here to stay and so is everyone else so you can drop your stupid racism argument and accept the fact that we are all here trying to live and do something.

Let's keep it real and agree that it was the Europeans who brought prosperity and modern civilization. They created the opportunity for the greatest nation in the world. The framework is genius but again, humans are stupid. I mean, just look at our current leaders. We have some of the greatest minds attempting to move our society forward, while the worst minds are leading us backwards.

Black people made it possible for all of us to have a constitutional chance to live equally and enjoy the prosperity and that should be enough for all of us to capitalize on here. There are people that do not want us to thrive and gain power and we must recognize that truth. Let's say they consider us ignorant. Can it be that the elites know something that we do not?

We know that the government lies to us. I mean, look at Roswell, New Mexico, and September 11th. Now, they admit UFOs are real after years of denying it but look at how many people still do not believe. The truth is our ignorance is a direct result of man-made religion. Christianity, Catholicism, and Islam are all promoting ignorance. So, who benefits from our ignorance if not the people who are pushing it?

The leaders of the Church know the truth and benefit from keeping it from us. It is a business and I will mention it once again because it is so important to know that at one time in our history the church would kill you if you believed otherwise. You either believed the lies or you would die. The Church converted the world by promoting their ignorance and at the same time, erasing the ancient knowledge of our ancestors. They literally erased history, denied reality, and forced their will for power and greed to create this man-made civilization.

In essence, they have cut the world off from the truth and tried to take the place of the Gods and what the Gods had taught our people. They cannot answer how and why these megalithic structures were created and are so sophisticated or how those who created those structures seem to know things that our modern scientists are barely just finding out now. If they were on that 12,000 years ago, imagine where they would have been now while we are barely there today?

Almost all the ancient societies believed in Alien Goddesses and Gods as if they knew them as real beings with real power. The proof is in the structures that were left behind that are still standing. Made in such ways that they are barely able to do today. Teotihuacan is called the city of the Gods because the Aztecs said that the God's are who created it. The mainstream scientists are idiots, and they get proven wrong all the time because they are assuming things through their man-made philosophies. They think that they are smart, and they think that they know everything. In doing so, they have closed their minds to the truth.

Evolution got pushed hard on the world without actual proof and people got rich off of that. Most mainstream scientists do not believe in the Bible and rightfully so, but they are also inaccurate as it denies reality. Their opinions become biased because they are based on what their minds are capable of thinking. Before you picked up this book, you might never have known the truth behind the music and the movies demonstrated here.

I have mentioned that it is true, especially when the Catholics destroyed ancient civilizations and histories so it appears that our modern scientists and everyone in our modern age appears to be operating on limited knowledge. Wouldn't it be more productive for our society if we stayed open to the truth? Some of you might not be able to even fathom what it is like to be a player in the game and how it really works, but we have the facts to back up what I am saying through our movies and our music. Real life is crazier than the songs and movies.

They are not exact truths, but if you know what to look for, you can get the messages. Why we have to know our business and these mainstream scientists will never know their business unless they truly include our ancient ancestor's history. The fucked-up part is that these mainstream ideas and opinions are being taught as facts and that closes off any arguments just like Christianity. That is complete ignorance. Our minds are so powerful so why close them? When I was in the hood kicking it with my homies in Planada, California, I could not even fathom how deep this game got, even though my older homies would warn me and tell me about this shit.

In the 90's, in California, my homies were tripping over satellites, plus we had curfews. If you were under eighteen years old, you could not be out past 10pm. We had check points where every car that left the hood got checked for warrants. Does that sound like a free country to you? Doesn't that sound like some gestapo tactics? This shit has been happening in the hood. I mean, the entire world is on drugs and the government still does not legalize it. Instead, they police us to death.

I could not even fathom this game and it almost got me killed. A lot of people cannot even fathom the media lying to them or losing their constitutional rights or a police officer killing them, let alone the government betraying them. That is exactly what will get them killed. So, stay sharp. Shouldn't it be enough that someone can think it can happen to make it possible for it to happen? Can we manifest a better future for Americans? If we can all agree it is our constitutional rights as Americans to pursue happiness and a better future for our country, then it is achievable.

Now, lets talk about manifestation for a little bit. We got our subconscious minds, and it is said that our subconscious is what leads and manifests our lives. I meditate and try to astral project and try to reach higher states of consciousness. My ultimate goal is to levitate. Have I come close to levitating? Fuck no, but no one has taught me or brought me books on it. If someone can please contact me for any reason or help or if you have any questions or just want to meet me, my information will be available at the end of this book. I have astral projected one time, so I know it is real. Some people believe that the manifestation of objects is real, but I do not know. Lets see if it is?

If manifestation were true, don't you think they would have manifested Jesus by now? Then again, what if the events that are predicted to happen are triggers that have to happen before he can be manifested? If manifestation was truly real, shouldn't they have manifested something real by now? Moses had a staff that turned into a snake or a real angel talking to someone in Israel. Instead, the Israeli defense minister claims to be in contact with Aliens.

We now know UAPs are real. It makes sense then when our ancient ancestors said that their God's and Goddesses came from the stars. That makes more sense than what this man-made religion says about their God. Maybe the fact that it is a man-made religion based on selective information, half-truths, and lies is the reason that they cannot manifest Jesus.

What if our hunger and thirst for our constitutional rights and freedoms to pursue truth happiness and enlightenment were based on truths? Then why can't we manifest it? Couldn't we truly and successfully preserve our human race and achieve everything that we can think of? Just because we cannot think of how to do something right now, it does not mean it is not possible. Or that it won't be thought of later.

Okay, so let us say that the Aliens and the government do not want us to know the truth and we are left with what we know and do not yet know? Through meditation and a drug, I was able to achieve such a high state of consciousness that I felt like I was transcending into a higher being, but my mortal body kept me here. If we know how to look, we can discover what were looking for.

Chapter 4

Let us talk about learning. If our minds are our most powerful weapon, then learning should be the most important priority for our society. We should be incredibly involved in every school system and demanding real courses to take us into the future. Math, science, ancient history, American history, music, sports, and serving in the military from 18 years old to 20 years old. This way we can learn survival and combat skills to defend ourselves. Why not?

We all need to be apart of something and it builds a community for each other. America can be dangerous, but it does not have to be, but when it is, people will be ready for it. Why is it that I rarely ever read a book that actually teaches me something? Every time I read a book; it is common sense shit that we already know. I was in college and all the books told me about was terminology. What a waste of time.

Why can't we learn the terms while applying the skills to the subject? Doing something physically is the best way to learn something. A lot of things can get you killed but having a short memory is a big problem. This is real life, and we should always pay attention to everything around us. Question everything that you see and hear. In this life, you cannot trust anyone, and everything has a meaning.

Look at television and how fake the people are. They cannot keep it real for shit because most of them are selling out looking and sounding dumb as fuck. That is all entertainment, and they will say anything and do anything for fame and money. The problem is that they all feel like they have something to say, like how Lebron James and the NBA defend China's crimes against humanity yet hate on our country.

These artists, actors, and sports starts are allowing their true characters to show. Send those idiots to serve in the military so they can do something for the country. If they do not like it, then they should shut their mouths. Stick to acting, music, and sports. Stay out of politics because they are all misinformed. Money does not make us, and you can go on about it all you want but at the end of the day, their still fake as fuck.

They should dump the democrats. Politics has perverted every part of television for the worst. I hate American television. It is so fake, and it does not represent our true culture. It is so ugly on television when most of the women around me are so beautiful. It is like they are having an ugly contest on T.V. As individuals, we need to learn our strengths and our weaknesses so we can capitalize on them.

A Goddesses beauty and qualities are one of their greatest weapons. Women are a noticeably big part of our lives, and it is no wonder the Queen is the most powerful piece on a chess board. This is why drugs and sex work should be legal. Legalizing it would make it safer for women and our communities. We have to protect women. It is the oldest profession, and you think people would have learned by now that it will never go away. Aliens thought women were so beautiful that they slept with them. They showed women how to use makeup.

Wouldn't legalizing drugs and sex work stop drug and sex trafficking? We change the laws for one victim but cannot change the laws for half the U.S. population? How many women have to die or how many overdoses have to happen before they realize the truth? Let us talk about the shows, "Law and order," and "the first 48." That shit is so fake. In Washington State, you have no rights to a fair trial.

There is no such thing and this whole thing we see on tv where they do not get enough on someone, so they have to let them go never happens. They will hold you and file trumped up charges so that they can charge you with lesser ones. They fabricate charges on you and make them sound worse than it really is. The state always picks up the chargers as it is literally framed as a business here in Washington. This is the government at its best.

It was on the news years ago about a couple that had just gotten married, and the bride dropped the bouquet, and the mom went to pick it up, but the bride pushed her out of the way so that she could pick it up. Police saw that and arrested the bride. They handout charges like its candy and trump up the charges so they can report the numbers and statistics at the end of the year to receive funding and equipment which is used to militarize the police.

A Romanian friend of mine claims that people are more oppressed here than in Romania which was a communist country. You cannot go one day without seeing a police officer. I am talking about them taking shit to the extreme. So, they tax high, and mass incarcerate, and it took a pandemic and riots with protests to even start a conversation…but nothing is happening. Gangsta Feat Bizzy Bone of Bone Thugs N Harmony & Lostcause by Londown

This fool did a beer run and the store owner chased him, so he threw a rock at him, and they charged him with armed robbery. These are not just rare examples. This is shit we are all going through. I got 70 months in prison for an argument. Shit, I had a job and was doing good. Want to talk about Nazi gestapo or communist regimes and systematic racism? Washington State is leading the way in all of those.

If you look at my record, it says that I am a kidnapper, assault in the second degree and a murderer but it is not true. Even the possession of controlled substance charge was because they found an empty bag of cocaine in my trash can. The shit I did do was always covered up by the police officers after I got my turf. This whole case is circumstantial as there is literally no weapon or witnesses. We need to change, for real. I was going to college and working under the table.

In my case, there was a journal that said all kinds of false shit about me, and it was proven to be false. It claimed that I was sleeping with a girl that I barely knew and when they asked her about it, she confirmed it was not true and that all the shit in this journal was made up. They still charged me with second degree assault, because the journal said that I had pulled a knife on someone. They charged me for that shit and then later they would drop those charges and then charge me with these murders.

This guy, two blocks away from the area, has seen someone but could not point me out in a photo line up two times, but then two years later, they bring him in for in-court identification after talking to the detectives and seeing me on the news. This so-called witness had already cooperated with the state and testified against his co-defendant on another murder case so that he could get a deal.

After not being able to point me out that night or the next day, but all of the sudden, two years later, he was able to point me out? This is why I hate those fucking shows man, they are so fake, and people watch that shit and believe that is how it is in real life, but it is not. We are getting policed to death with no action at liberty. It is supposed to be better to have a guilty man go free under the law than to lock up innocent people. Before trial they sent me to Eastern State Hospital to get me competent for trial. All they did was have me watch Law & Order and 12 angry men.

In their eyes, everyone is guilty. It should not be the duty of police officers to take care of all of our problems. You see what is happening in Ukraine with Russia invading. Ukraine is asking for everyone who is capable of fighting to fight for their country. Look at our leaders selling us out and if we get invaded, the government will go underground while we are left to defend ourselves. If everyone served in the military, then every civilian would be able to defend our homes against foreign or domestic government threats.

Could you imagine if we got invaded? What would cops do? Would they seek asylum, or would they be fighting with us? Cops are so quick to kill civilians and arrest innocent people that it is hard to imagine them actually fighting for this country. Some would definitely fight for us but if we got taken over by a dictator, the cops are the ones they will use to take over our country. A cop's willingness to enforce most of these ridiculous laws, violating our constitutional rights, plus their willingness to kill civilians speaks for itself.

Look how quick the government was to pull the trigger on emergency laws during the pandemic and how the leaders were not following their own laws. Yet, civilians were getting arrested every day. Once again, it is someone abusing their powers. Politicians should not have immunity and they should be held to the same standards as the lowest classes in our society. A chain is only as strong as its weakest link.

Politicians should be paid minimum wage plus benefits and that is it. Give them a house rent free, but all other bills and taxes must be paid. In order to fix problems and relate, you must know your business. After they get veted to become a politician. That is why it makes no sense trying to push a one world order when they cannot even fix all of our country's problems.

Most Americans are happy with a normal house, marriage, kids, and a car with a 9 to 5 job, having fun, and enjoying the outdoors, urban lifestyles, doing drugs and drinking alcohol for recreational purposes. What is wrong with that? We all earn our right to pursue true happiness. But in order for us to know true happiness, we must truly learn what makes us happy. We will never know unless we try it. Who are they to tell us what makes us happy or what we should do? If you harm none then do what you will.

I have dealt with a lot of racism at work, so I have always wanted to start my own business. That is what I went to college for and what I will do if I get out. I would definitely donate to St. Jude and bank with Wells Fargo. Cancer is a tragic problem, and it should not be a reason not to live our lives, but it should be a reason for us to unite and use all of our resources and capabilities to find a cure. That would be tax money well spent.

They want to give other terrorist states billions of dollars of our money and spend millions on domestic infrastructure to change names and words in our vocabulary when they should be spending it on things that truly matter. These democrats cannot even balance their own books because they embezzle it and spend money unwisely, so they rely on government funds.

That should be illegal. That is why they want more and more taxes. They use the Rico act on regular street gangs, but the politicians are really the ones involved in organized racketeering like Hilliary Clinton and Joe Biden. If they do not use the Rico act on these crooked politicians, then they should not use it on Americans. Crime should be dealt with as a community and police officers should be a part of the community.

If drugs and sex work were legal, it would reduce a lot of violence and deaths and that is a fact. You might have drug induced crimes which becomes mental issues. Instead of money, power, and greed it would make blue collar and white-collar crimes based on money and greed. It is exactly what our politicians are doing today.

We should invest our tax money on the superhuman schools seen in the documentary by Caroline Cory. It is called, "Superhuman: The invisible made visible." It is so exciting to see what the mind is capable of, and we have a duty to nurture this growth as a nation. So, if, theoretically, we can think it then we can achieve it even if we cannot fathom how at the time of thought. In theory, all of the shit in this book is possible if we can agree.

The politicians and their few followers can disagree all they want but the truth is that they have already proved that they are not fit to lead. We know that most of the media and newspapers sold out and lie for these people except for a few news outlets like Fox News but even they can be biased. Tucker Carlson from Fox News should be an example of what a journalist should be doing period. Joe Rogan is doing more for the truth than the media.

We should make truth our religion and learn by questioning everything. Don't they say the truth shall set you free? There is always going to be crime, but drugs, sex work, and poverty should not have to be the reason.

Chapter 5

Let us talk religion and why it is so important to know the truth. Christianity is not our history nor is the Bible a complete set of books. Christians destroyed most of our ancestral history and forced their beliefs on the world, you will even see churches on ancient holy sites. We talked about this earlier, but Satanism is a form of Christianity as it comes from Christian beliefs, so I call them Christians as well. Shit, I have met Satan worshippers who are nicer than some so called Christians but what I mean is that they are both from the same pantheon and beliefs.

You can still agree with the principals but that is all it is. Do not expect Jesus to protect you just like you should not count on a cop to be there for you. The Bible is filled with a lot of human wisdom but you should read all the books so you can get a full understanding of what it is really saying. There are so many religions around the world that were created by our ancestral alien Gods that taught our ancestors knowledge that our modern-day scientists are just barely starting to understand. Their are books out their by S.L. MacGregor Mathers Alelster Crowley etc that can show you how to do everything the Bible says Jesus Christ did. Many people have transcended and reached these higher paths. Almost all our ancient ancestors had a way to achieve such heights. As our ancestors were taught by different Gods. Have you Read Tranceformation of America by Cathy O'Brien & Mark Phillips. That book shocked me because this shits so crazy on these streets Their so powerful I would call them God. You know what I mean. Its insane. I knew this Russian Military Vet from the Afghan war and he showed me some very powerful tech that is being used on us everyday and we wouldnt even know it. He asked me in such a way to make it a point what he was showing me. He asked me to listen to this song and showed me the name of it called Eye boogers and it was in Russian so I didn't understand a word it said. Whatever right? The next day after I woke up I had eye crust but the crazy part is I had eye crust all day. It did not stop. I was so concerned I was trying vizine to try to stop it. It's never happened to me before and all I could think of was the song he showed me. Were talking about our minds here. T.V., Music Movies, have they found a way to hijack our minds? What is Christianity really saying? The Lamb of God. Rapture. What are we supposed to be? Meat for the Gods? Have you seen the Movie Jupiter Ascending. If you study these historical books then you know its said the Ancient Gods of the Abyss feed on blood such as the Feathered Serpent the Azetcs worshiped. The Living Gods such as Enki, you offer Bread. Before you enter the first gate the gatekeeper must give you a name. I think about that because I smoked some PCP one time and I entered this state of being and enlightenment and I wanted to know. Who am I? What am I? Why am I here? The mystery here is why couldnt i answer these basic questions in that realm state? It seems like we have another part of our minds that must be taught. These questions come to us out of a very real need in our lives. It's a very natural part of our human potential. Their is a whole universe out their and you think working for the man is more important? We have the very essence of Gods in us. Antichrist Pt 2 by Conejo I know so well and is so true. According to the Grand Grimoire of Mr. Venitiliana Del Rabina Satan a God.

These are facts but some people think Jesus was the antichrist as he was the son of man, therefore, Christians worship a man and they killed off the ancient divine religions of the Gods in his name. Yahweh is God's name, meaning, "I am," in Hebrew. So, then you are essentially saying that you are a God if you worship Yahweh. I believe in Yahweh myself. So, in the Anunnaki history according to the book, "The 12th planet," by Zecharia Sitchin, Enki and his sister created us to mine for gold with the order having come from Anu and Enlil.

Enki taught humans knowledge and in the book of Enoch, it was the watchers who taught the humans. In India, they have their Gods and Native Americans have the star people. The Aztecs claimed that they came from underground as the God's created them there we know now their talking about the big dipper. Christianity wants you to believe that the son of man is a God. We know that Jesus performed miracles allegedly, but he never rose from the dead. So, humans created a man-made religion and elevated themselves to God status and tried erasing the ancient divine knowledge of the Alien Gods from our history and cutting us off from contact.

Now, everyone is acting brand new and shit. Look how stupid our leaders are. They cannot even fathom alien Gods let alone the UAP technology. Our military would not even stand a chance if the aliens wanted to destroy us. We are here because the Gods created us. According to the Anunnaki, Enlil was going to let us all die in the Great Flood, but Enki saved the humans that he and his sister created because we were their great creation, so he gave us a chance to survive.

A lot of our ancient history has the same kind of stories all around the world, So, maybe the Gods allowed our ignorant species to live because we do have the capabilities to achieve the great potential of our minds. This is why we must learn the truth.

I worship the Moon Goddess of Wales beautiful as she has pale white skin, blond hair, moon eyes and is divinely perfect. In the Anunnaki history, it is said that the Anunnaki liked to be called Gods but that they were not immortal. They died just like us, but they lived far longer than humans do. If this is true, then that would make us truly inferior to aliens and maybe that is why we are obsessed with immortality. The same way a human can have a couple of dogs in their lifetimes, an alien can see generations of our lifetimes.

It makes sense when the defense minister of Israel said that Aliens believe that we are not ready. I mean, the United States is a global superpower and look at our leaders. Look at our problems. Everyone is on about some stupid shit. Even if some of us are playing chess while others are playing checkers, they are playing alien god games that we can barely fathom. Our top scientists can, in theory, understand how these claims our ancestors made about Gods can be possible, but the aliens are already doing it. It's said that their 50 years ahead of what we can fathom.

The government was not aware that we can be in contact as the defense minister from Israel claimed, but they are definitely not telling us what is going on and that is a fact. We are not ready they say but let us contemplate why they say that. I have been telling you that we cannot trust anyone out here. Now, let me tell you something, if you are running a business, club, or gang or anything else would you let someone in whom you cannot trust? Maybe, they do not trust us. They do not trust our leaders and we should not trust them either.

We should not trust them for human reasons. They lie to us. What if the Gods think humans are ignorant and our leaders think that we are ignorant? We cannot deny truth and reality. Everyone has short memories and is going on about something man-made. This is the greatest country in the world and so-called Americans want to bring it down and our leaders want to sell us out and create a one world order like they are worthy of leading the world.

Truth is, unless we change our path, our leaders and unrighteous people are going to run this country into the ground. If you are a real player, you will understand that it is always someone close to you that will try to bring you down. We do this shit for real and have been through it a few times and just when you think you have seen it all, it just gets worse.

I am ready for the aliens. I want the Pleiades God and Goddesses to come back. I want to know what happened to them. So, back in the day, if you believed in aliens, Christians would kill you. I know for a fact that the government is working with the Church. Why our constitution is so important but the democrats are weaponizing all the institutions? Democrats are the government, and all of these idiots are just eating their lies up. Republicans in the past have been known to push this one world order also.

Dump the one world order and hold on to our constitution and guns. Why we are in this together as a lot of people do not care and cannot even fathom this shit? All we can do is stay true and keep seeking the truth and hopefully keep each other informed so please feel free to contact me and pass this on to the right people. Do not even trip, I am going to be right here and bang it out with whoever has a problem hearing the truth. From what I know and seen in my experience working the field I feel like these mass shootings are being provoked by our government. All you need is someones e-mail address and you have almost total control of their phone. They technologicaly terrorize, harass and track you. Research this shit because they have tech to make someone do things. like subliminal messages but Its more direct and blunt. You get mentaly engaged and only you and they know. Its what this is all about because unless your in the know you cant see it. Guns have always been around way before us and its never been this bad. Guns are not the problem its the individual. Why all of a sudden are individuals acting up? Most these fools have it way better than we did growing up and their all acting like they got it worse. Why? They have this program called community policing and they use all this shit Im talking about on gangmembers etc. They stalk you and their goal is to get you back in prison if your not working. Its crazy and very real. You have military activity in plain sight happening around you everyday.

Chapter 6

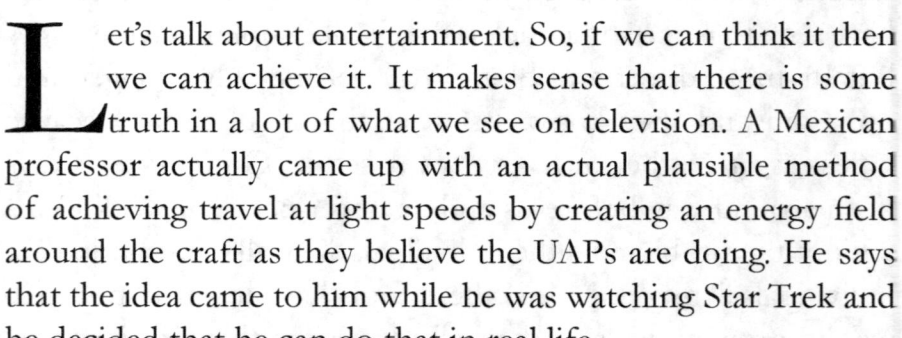

Let's talk about entertainment. So, if we can think it then we can achieve it. It makes sense that there is some truth in a lot of what we see on television. A Mexican professor actually came up with an actual plausible method of achieving travel at light speeds by creating an energy field around the craft as they believe the UAPs are doing. He says that the idea came to him while he was watching Star Trek and he decided that he can do that in real life.

It makes sense. There are actually a lot of amazing and genius movies and anime stories that we can learn from. Truly amazing work as these concepts are based on real, plausible, human emotions, behavior, and potential. The animated, "Rick and Morty," captures the power of the mind beautifully. What if some laws are universal in nature? Like, you see in Star Trek, Star Wars, anime, and movies like Men In Black. What if there are pieces of shit in every race, civilization, and Empire? For as smart as Rick and Morty claim to be in the end their just a couple of sellouts promoting demorat agenda.

The ancient history of the Gods reveals their imperfect characters and behaviors. This is why we should not be racist with each other as every race will have serial killers, child molesters, and rapists. Those are crimes against innocent women and children and should be condemned by all races as they are preying on the helpless.

Not all murders are wrong, I mean, look at the cops. They kill people all the time and they justify it. We want accountability for when they kill innocent people when a taser or simply talking to someone could have been used to defuse the situations. We need our self-defense rights back. This behavior may be universal, and it is in our ancient history.

Look at the Greek Gods fighting, and they are mostly related to each other. Look at the movie called, "The Man in the Iron Mask," with Leonardo Decaprio and how he was imprisoned by his own brother for power. We know that it is a fact from history and people like Hitler, Stalin, and these modern-day politicians like Hilary Clinton, Joe Biden, George Bush, Anderw Cuomo, and so many more examples show just how corrupt man can be. Why wouldn't we put our leaders through a test and vet them? Why would we just give anyone power and money? These career Politicians are nothing then become rich after getting elected.

We know for a fact that not just anyone is fit to lead and the fact that some of these people want to be a politician should be enough to question their motives and their loyalties. The reasons why they want to become a politician is not enough to justify just handing someone the keys to the country. We question to some degree, but tests should definitely be given to prevent our leaders from abusing power.

One of my favorite sports shows was called, "Speak for yourself," with Wiley and Acho because they are a perfect example of how society is and should be. Wiley is a genius as he sees life in a way that is color blind and humane. He keeps it real with his logic and his views are based on his truths while Acho is always going on about something and putting race in the mix.

People need to speak for themselves to be able to learn from each other because we know that every race has its garbage and if we say that we speak for our people then you are representing that garbage too. This black guy was on the news for randomly punching a five-year-old kid and there is so many stories like that. Straight up bitch shit but to say that all black people are like that is just not true, so, it is better to speak for ourselves.

A lot of rappers spit some real game in their music, and it has a real effect on people and can influence many. There was a time when I did not understand what it was that I was hearing but it would sound tight, so I would bump that shit. Obviously, if we listen to sad music, we are going to be feeling sad. Being sad is not cool but people can relate and listen to it to help them get through some of the tough times in their lives. People use music to feel better or some kind of way, but they are just feelings and after the song is over, reality hits again and we are still in the same spot.

We must understand everything that we are listening to. What it means and what is being said and how it pertains to and happens in real life. We must understand music, movies, television shows, and books in the same way that we seek the truth in our lives. This is so we can learn, overcome our mistakes, and break the cycles in our lives.

I believe that Christianity has a lot to do with domestic violence in relationships, as it teaches how it believes a relationship should be sacred. If that is what we are taught and believe then if it is not all perfect and someone cheats, it feels like a total betrayal by your partner. That is a totally man-made concept, and it is unrealistic to ask of someone unless they truly feel that way. Domestic violence would be reduced so much if relationships and sex were taught to be just a natural part of life.

The Anunnaki believed it was enough to sleep with someone if both involved felt the same urges in their loins for each other. Not to take from marriage, but the truth is that any marriage can work if we do not have these unrealistic ideas and expectations. The truth is that you should not have to do anything that you do not want to. We must truly know ourselves and our partners.

A lot of people listen to rap and think that they are crazy and that they know what is going on from watching movies and television shows, but then they get themselves into real life shit and get knocked off their stools when they find out that the real world is nothing like the movies. A lot of people get killed because of that shit.

These idiots who are promoting socialism, Marxism, and globalism here in America do not know what they are talking about. Why don't they go and live in a country that is like that already instead of going on about that shit here? Theirs always gonna be someone feeling the need to entertain the spirits. By teaching us the truth and sending everyone to serve in the military, we would be saving so many innocent lives and ensuring a strong future and society.

We also see a lot of movies on artificial intelligence and technology. If we can create artificial intelligence to be superior to humanity now, then why shouldn't we use that to advance our race? For instance, we know element 115 exists but we cannot make it stable. We know from Bob Lazar that it can be stabilized and that we need element 115 to power crafts and to create an energy field. Why don't we task artificial intelligence to come up with the solutions for us? Buzzlightyear movie?

Scientists say that we would need the power of a black hole to do certain things and yet we have proof that it can be done by seeing what these UAPs are doing already. So, it is not that it cannot be done but rather that us humans cannot do it. The UAPs are using the energy of the Earth. In using artificial intelligence, shouldn't it be the way we compute the question to artificial intelligence how we get our answers? We have to make artificial intelligence a sort of MacGyver for all of our known resources to achieve our goals.

We should have artificial intelligence create and solve each problem one at a time. In essence, is artificial intelligence not the very essence of science and truth? We would have to supply artificial intelligence with all of our true and proven theories and knowledge of all known materials for it to truly be effective. This would allow for artificial intelligence to take us into these other dimensions of knowledge that we, right now, cannot comprehend. Instead these techies are creating AI to manipulate Humans.

Some of my favorite shows are on the Fox News channel, like the Gutfeld show. Kat Timpf is so perfectly beautiful especially when she does not have hair extensions on. Dana

Perino is a true divineGoddess. Fox News is the most honest on television and report on the government all the time. What aggravates me, however, is that they report the news, but nothing happens to the people that they report on. Look at Andrew Cuomo and all the shit that he did. It took several women to finally stand up to him for his ass to get in any kind of trouble. We must hold these so-called leaders accountable as a community and support each other. The truth is so important in everything we do, and we need to question everything.

If you have ever heard of or seen the show, "Ancient Aliens," you will notice in their introduction, they say that we must question everything as that is the most important thing that you can do, and it does not matter what people think especially if you know the truth and they do not. The mainstream scientists and their followers that are assuming that they know everything want to make others feel inferior. The reason they want to do this is because they actually think that they are superior which is truly the ultimate ignorance. They are constantly getting proven wrong but having gotten fame and money for it for so long, they cannot be reasoned with.

A lot of actors and artists in the industry as well as politicians are doing the same thing. They are saying anything and everything for money and fame. Look at how dumb some of these artists really are. If you stop and think about it, there is really nothing cool about them. The noises they make sound primitive, like a brainless animal. Their clothing is just ridiculous, and they join together. If you do not like their shit, then they try to make you feel bad which is a natural reaction to rejection.

Do people like it, yes, and it can be fun, but is it productive? For the artist it is but not for society. It is okay to have fun and again, we all need to speak for ourselves. I personally do not think that there is anything cool about skinny jeans, but fashion is a personal choice, and we should wear what we want to. We all should have our own styles that we like and do it right. My weapons had to look nice and new. You would never catch me with a cheap ass burner. I had to have nice equipment and I would never go anywhere without a strap. If I could go out without a strap, I would have but we must make it possible to be that way.

I love complex stories and the Japanese culture as I used to work with them. I have seen World War II movies and have learned about our history. A lot of times, we must fight someone before we become friends and I feel like that is what happened between our countries. Don't you think they have learned from their mistakes, and we should be able to move forward? We should give the Japanese their swords back as allies and unleash their true potential in Asia.

We saved China from Japan, and now look, China has become too big for its own good with all of its crimes against Americans and humanity. Shouldn't we allow Japan to counter China's aggression? We can take some good from television if we dissect, question, and analyze what we watch as we should be doing in everything we do. Otherwise, it is a complete waste of time. We must entertain ourselves with intriguing things and ideas to elevate ourselves.

Do you think that aliens have televisions? In the show, "Rick and Morty," there is galactical televisions and world porn. It is a good question. What would alien television look like and what do you think they think when they see our television? Can you imagine how we look or come off to them? What do they think about us?

Lebron James is doing something, but he has got no style. He plays like he is so stiff that he can barely wipe his ass. Michael Jordan did everything with style and finesse. We can say that Michael is classy and Lebron is trashy. If we are being observed, wouldn't we as a society want to act like we are being observed like our ancestors did? It said that even when your alone we must act as if the walls have eyes,

Okay, I am a Las Vegas Raiders fan even though it is so hard to love them and watch them play. Its good were trying a new quarterback, just win baby. So, I am not knocking anyone else's hustle because making money is what our country is about, but I mention shit so that we can distinguish entertainment from our reality. I really enjoy British television, especially their murder mysteries which I find them to be master pieces. They do shit properly. The thing with the streets and entertainment is that when shit pops off, everyone has something to say, and you will hear all of the chatter that is going on about shit, but they do not even know what is really going on or what time it is.

It is like talking shit about a movie they are watching but they have no clue what it is really about. Some of these rappers are trying to creep, slither, and crawl like they are doing something. The problem with the serpent's blood is that it can never endure because it is cold blooded. They run out of heat fast, so they are only good for a few strikes before they run out of juice. They pretty much can only catch you by surprise. Their songs last for what? Two or three minutes of funk and then they are done. Next thing you know, they are singing and crying about their problems. Some of us have got real big problems that you would not wish on anyone.

Trying to explain the game to someone is like trying to get an animal to choose shapes. Only some can do it. What does that mean when our minds are so sharp? We have to stay true to the game. Listen to this song called, "Friends, Friends, Friends," by Mz Gatiz featuring Lil Cuete when he says that we are getting sicker than the illuminati. You have to understand what that means.

It is for your own good that we question everything. A lot of people like to ask what this has to do with them. The thing is that if you truly value your life you should care, because George Floyd and all of the innocent victims could be you. I remember when cops were beating my homie up and I went to jump in, so they ended up beating all of our asses. There is nothing like being powerless. That show, "Holmes Family Rescue," is a good one because they are stand up and solid in their business and that means something. That is a rare thing in any business, and we need leaders like that in politics.

CHAPTER 7

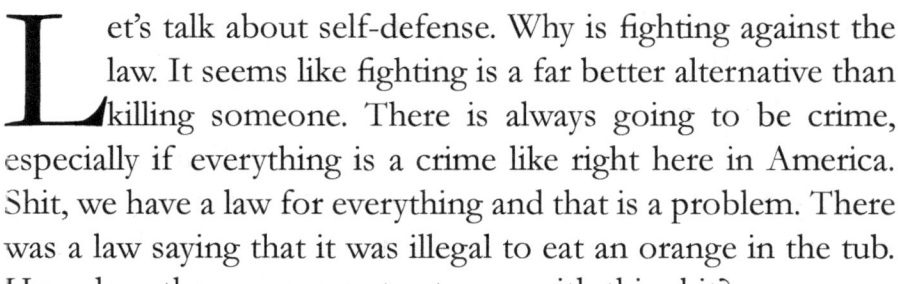

Let's talk about self-defense. Why is fighting against the law. It seems like fighting is a far better alternative than killing someone. There is always going to be crime, especially if everything is a crime like right here in America. Shit, we have a law for everything and that is a problem. There was a law saying that it was illegal to eat an orange in the tub. How does the government get away with this shit?

The truth is that laws are necessary for companies and society, but they need to be in accordance with common sense and reality. We really need to reset our federal and state laws. Look at the pandemic and how they really had no idea how to deal with things and relied on irresponsible idiots like Dr. Fauci and W.H.O. They were completely lying to everyone instead of following the science. How did they make half of the world look? Fauci and W.H.O in a cover up playing people like idiots. While the rest suffer for their Ignorance. The problem is that we as a country cannot afford them to make these mistakes on theese levels. In a football game you can do that shit. On that level its professional and pure buisness so why are they in office? Anybody can lie and guess what to do. Teachers should get paid by their performances and ethics. Why are teachers asking for more money if our countrys GPA is below Avg? At this point They should be fired. Im union member 133% but when it comes to Education the teachers union needs to put a performance clause on all their contracts. Their obligated to teach professionally. Restrict the SBA's authority to just regulate teachers performances. What else is school for?

Since the beginning of time, there has been fighting and murder. If soldiers and police officers are allowed to use force to defend themselves then why aren't civilians who are also dealing with their own kinds of dramas in the communities allowed to defend ourselves? No one deserves to be the victim of hate, bullies, or crime but it is an unpleasant fact of life. Defending ourselves should also be a fact of life.

I remember a marine picked a fight with me during a barbeque. He tried to grab my throat and balls at the same time, trying to handicap me. I pushed him off of me and knocked him out with one punch and kicked him in the head. I stopped after that, but not only did I get arrested but the cop wanted to beat my ass because my adrenaline was so high that I was going through emotions. If that dumb ass would not have touched me, none of that shit would have happened. That is bullshit and why it is not enough to just talk about police reform. We need true justice reform.

I did nine months in jail for that shit, plus I lost my job and everything. If we have a constitutional right to life, happiness, and liberty, then shouldn't our laws reflect our principals? So, if we are all living our lives and enjoying our creator Gods liberties, shouldn't our laws be based on this foundation? Common sense and humane laws for our society are what we need. I like to drink and do drugs for spiritual and recreational purposes and if someone else does not like to do that, as long as no one is forcing you, it should not be a problem.

Some people do not want the vaccine and do not want to wear a mask. If we want to smoke in a restaurant, that should be the owner's decision. If people do not like it, they can go somewhere else where the owner does not allow it. So, we know that the pandemic and the lockdown caused major mental health issues. So, can we all agree that these ridiculous laws against our human nature in our country can be directly related to our mental health crime and poverty issues as well?

I mean, the very fact and purpose of laws is to try and make a perfect human like Jesus. There is no such thing, and it is against the natural laws of nature. We are truly oppressed as we are getting policed to death. A lot of these laws go against the natural order of humanity and progress in happiness, life, and mental development. It is clear that our politicians are living under different circumstances as they have immunity, and it clearly shows when we are forced to follow the laws that they make which they themselves cannot follow. This is just another example of how they are unfit to lead.

Why is it that some states allow self defense and others do not when it should be our constitutional right? Why is it that our leaders always try to water down our constitutional rights instead of improving them? That is another sign that they are unfit to lead. We know humans are not perfect and humans are the reason it has gotten this bad. Alien Gods are not perfect either according to their history. We know that our minds are very powerful and even if we do not know everything, we should always be striving to learn from our mistakes. Why is it said that God does not like a complainer and yet our leaders are changing laws and trying to change reality for people that are obviously trying to infringe on other people's happiness and lives by complaining?

Just like the mainstream scientists who believe that they know everything, and they assume that their views are correct. The truth is that there is only one truth to everything just different perceptions, and we must ask questions and work to understand what it is. It should matter whether we like it or not and we have to keep it real for the sake of our future. Is that not what the moral of the story about the boy who cried wolf is about? We must instill true character to prevent this kind of behavior.

Why do you think that some youngsters see a movie or hear a rap that they like and then think that they are with the business and when the truth about the life hits them, they rat or bitch out? By then, the damage is done, and half of their lives are wasted. A lot of these fools in prison are that way. We should not be encouraging this behavior either. Not even criminals want a dumb criminal.

Why shouldn't we pay close attention and invest the most in education and the military? WE do not want Kings and Queens, but rather Goddesses and Gods. Professional American Gods.

Some of these artists, athletes and actors are truly amazingly talented and that is very respectful but then you start hearing them talk about shit and their stupidity starts to show. The gymnast, Kennedi Davis, for the University of Washington is an example of a Goddess. She is divinely beautiful and just as talented as she does her routines elegantly and perfectly.

She suffered injuries but she is a Goddess in her sport as she knows her business and does it with class. Now, imagine her like that in every part of life. She can truly be worshipped by someone.

I truly enjoy British television shows of back in their day as they have proper civilized etiquette and manners. The Asians show their perfections in their Feng Shui and tea ceremonies. They make these simple things a work of art. Why can't we treat everything we value the same way? Our schools, laws, and ways of life. It is a shame when you hear about someone so passionate and adamant about something that you know is false. Have you ever tried talking to religious people or some mainstream journalist or a scientist?

There is a better help commercial on television and this girl is explaining to her father about all of her problems and he tells her to just smile. That is truly the kind of advice that you will get from people and that is how useless lies and false information are. So, why would you treat any theory as fact unless it can truly be proven?

In my case, the prosecutor was able to get me convicted with nothing but a theory in Washington State. No witness, no weapon, and no motive, just someone who was not even there who thought I might have had something to do with it. It makes no sense. If America was built on prosperity, then why are our laws not made with the same intent? Not by handouts or welfare, but opportunity for everyone.

Right now, American laws are exactly opposite of that and that is another reason that our leaders are unfit to lead. Our shit shows when we talk, and their shit shows in mostly everything that they have done. We are judged by what we say and do. That is common sense and people should not have to be told these things, but this ignorance is what greed, lies, and corruption create.

If people live out the Christian principals, that is fine but to pass it off as absolute and true is truly ignorant especially when the facts are that we cannot even fathom exactly what they are talking about. Reality is so much more complex and crazier. They feed us such garbage food in Washington state that I do not even know what is real meat and what is soy meat anymore. I have been eating this shit for so long that I can no longer tell the difference. That is exactly what the government has done to our brains. People do not know what is true and real from what is a lie and what is fake anymore.

Ava Max the artist is so talented and beautiful that I would make satisfying her and pleasing her my religion. The truth is that most of us do not even know what truly pleases us or what makes us happy or how to be treated or treat someone else. The true test is, can we even explore the basic fundamental pleasures to find happiness under our current laws? The answer to that question is no. Even without harming others, are we able to achieve personal happiness? That is a violation of our constitutional rights and goes against our humanity.

We were not created to live in prison, but they would rather create prisons and mass incarcerate the population then to change the laws. Why are drugs and sex work illegal? The truth is that there is no reason other than someone's personal beliefs that it's bad, even though a lot of the population believes differently and beliefs are a personal choice. We must operate under the knowledge of science, wisdom and truth. Most of our laws stem from the Christian beliefs of creating and trying to be a perfect man. It is a fact that there is no such thing as a perfect man. Why Jesus? Why not ENKI. Seriously who really wants to be like Jesus?

Even within the scriptures, it is said that Jesus was the only one and that is only if you believe that. It is simply unrealistic and wrong to keep going about life this way. So, we cannot create the perfect man and that is a fact. Should we not then be trying to create the perfect laws for Americans? We can start by defining our contribution to our American society by working and serving in the military and our rights would be to procreate and be happy enjoying our lives as we strive into our futures. Work, life, and play. Try to achieve our Godhoods.

The problem with these policing issues is the legislature itself as it is their job to create laws, but instead, they are legislating us to death. We should reset their positions and laws to go about things differently. Their jobs should be to create the most common sense and humane laws that follow the progress and transition to keep up with our times future. We know that things work in seasons and in cycles. Therefore, it is our humane purpose in life to break out of our cycles. Shouldn't it be our leader's duty to break the incarceration cycles as well?

Drugs and sex work have been around since the beginning, and they are not going anywhere, so shouldn't we consider how to adapt to living with them instead of dealing with the stupid endless cycle of mass incarceration for those things? It is our duty to learn from our mistakes so that we do not repeat them but that applies to our natural laws of human nature. If we touch fire, we will get burned and then we learn not to do that again. So, it should be against the law to touch a fire. Why? Because it will burn you. What should the punishment be for doing so? You already got burned.

So, it would make sense that lighting peoples shit on fire should be illegal. Our laws should reflect our human nature, not our human choices that we make. Drugs can be addictive but to most Americans, the addiction is worth the pleasure and benefits that you get from being on drugs. Let some idiot fight for their right to touch a fire and we can honestly call them special. This woke concept is truly stupid as they are trying to go against the natural laws of human nature and deny reality. That shit does nothing for society's future.

If science permits transgender, that is fine, we should accept people who want to be different genders. So, why can't we legally enhance our DNA to its full potential? We must be open to all possibilities. Why don't we focus on how we can enhance our bodies and minds and unlock our greatest weapon?

Have you seen the movie, "Lucy," with Scarlet Johansen? It is a genius concept of the brain's potential. You know, it is a movie as they used the stupid Darwin's theory of evolution. Science proves our DNA was manipulated plus our ancient ancestors said that we were created by them. The idea that our brains are that powerful yet research shows that we only use a small percentage of it is truly a mystery. Why? Whats the missing element.

Chapter 8

Let us talk about why it is so important to dissect and question everything. A lot of this so-called scientific data as well as polls are funded by the companies and special interest groups that benefit from them, so of course they are going to make the numbers come out in their favor. Shit ends up being biased and therefore becomes irrelevant. That is exactly how information is being used today. It is dishonest and it is disrespectful to Americans. Now, they are all going on about misinformation and of course the business sector has been getting involved since they are the ones benefitting from these policies and the data.

Naturally, it will benefit them, but the truth is that they are funding these surveys. The drug companies are getting rich off of these vaccines so of course they want everyone to get vaccinated. I am vaccinated and I did it to avoid all of the covid problems to my health, but I have never caught coronavirus and I plan to keep it that way. I keep my distance from people naturally as I do not trust anyone. I practice silence so that I do not look or sound stupid going on about some shit.

It is best for me to stay focused by stopping, looking, and listening. I do not even know how many times I have been knee deep in some shit with someone trying to kill me and when I needed a homie, they would totally let me down. I have learned that the right people are going to come at the right time. That is why they are called players in the game. I have nothing but respect and love for the city of Los Angeles. The players their have class and are true to the game.

Las Vegas and San Franciso, as well as Ohio and Texas. The rapper Conejo's music is truly speaking the language and he knows the lingo. When he talks about his problems, you can relate because they are problems that are caused by being in the game. It was an honor to have Conejo and Bone thugs N harmony rap about me and for me. They are Gods in their own rights. Bone has been spitting that real game since day one. Then you got dumbass rappers like the Otha Side from Vallejo that do not even know what it is that they are talking about while trying to sound hard and acting like they are doing something. You could tell by what they are saying that they are not doing shit but talking and it is like that with mostly all rappers. Just professional shit talkers. I've seen blacks on T.V. my whole life and they are in every sport, show, school so why are we still hearing about racism?

Ice Cube, Dr. Dre, Snoop Dog, Jay Z and 50 Cent all have money and have become successful, but they will never know what it is like to work in the field. The song, "Pressure," by Joe Blow and Philthy Rich is really saying something about what it is really like out there on the streets. So why would you be all up in your chicken shit feelings and emotions showing weakness? A lot of people do not have the luxury of doing that shit. It is like, Justin Bieber singing a sad song even though he is rich and shit. That is like an oxymoron and people think that they are legit.

It is something when these actors that are known to be bad asses in the movies like, "Casino," or, "Rambo," or some shit then they always find a role to play a woman in a movie. Their actors and artists and they do it for money so why would you listen to them for any reason other than for entertainment? Some rappers are really with the business, and most are not but they act like they are, and it is like that in everything. That is why we must know our business.

Some movies are made with such detail that you can tell that they put a lot of thought into them, but if you ask a real war veteran if he likes war movies, a lot will tell you that they do not because it is not what it is really like. We keep it real because the truth is that it will not prepare you for it either. It is not enough to watch shit and then want to go and do it. You could want to be a football player but unless you put in the work and learn the business, you will never be a real football player. At best, you are playing flag football and there is nothing wrong with that, but you are not a pro player. The thing is, is that you could be if you really want to.

It is better to die then to enter these true realms with fear or doubt in your hearts. There must be perfect love and perfect trust in the truth.

To my fellow Gods and Goddesses, here are some of my personal thoughts and understandings according to my studies so far:

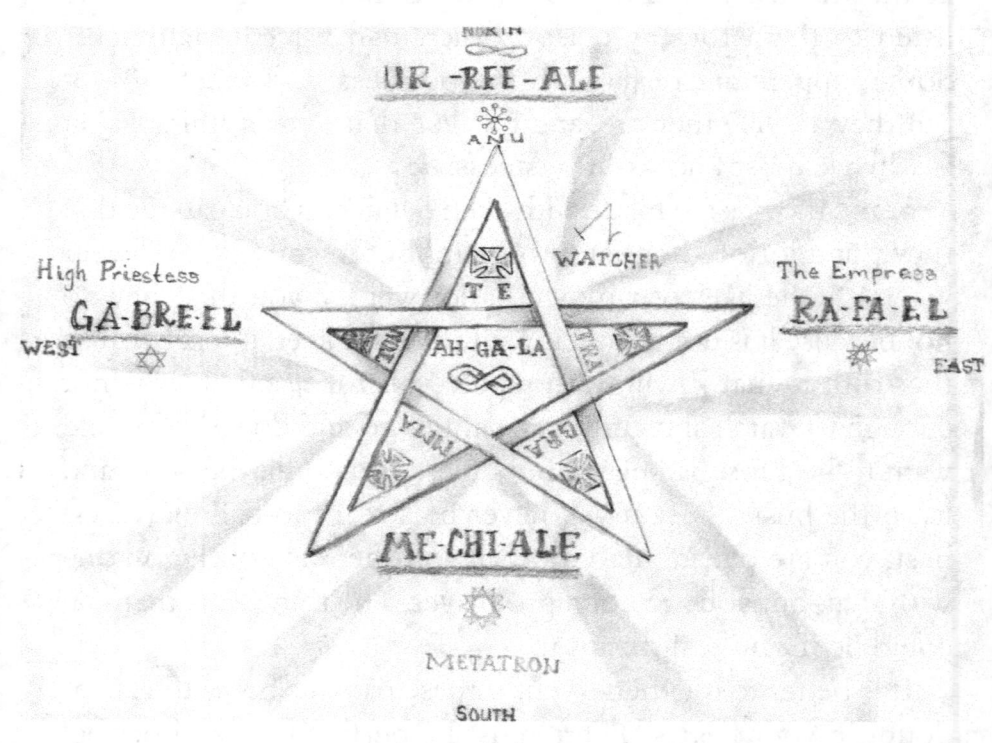

CHAPTER 9

NEPtune Thunders book of shadows and lights

East is RA-FA-EL Guardian of the world. Whose star is the double pentagram ten point star. To face the East is to speak to the Universe asking in the direction of our star. Using our star within us given to us by the TE-TRA-GRA-MMA-TON. When I lay down to await the answers the Archangel GABRE-EL is At my Crown. Guardian of the West whose star is the star of David. This is the Kingdom of the West.

The North and South are the Polar Kingdoms. My Left and Right. To my Left is the Archangel UR-REE-ALE Guardian of the North whose star is the eight rayed star. Where my Gods ENKI and ISHTAR came from. ENKI being our creators who gave us our sign of the human race and promised to protect us and return. He charged the Watcher to protect us and they are of a different race who used to fight on the side of the entitys of the Abyss but did not like their methods. So they are with ENKI.

To my right is the Archangel ME-CHI-ALE Guardian of the South whos star is the double star/crown of David. 12 point star the Metatron star of Enoch. The serpent wisdom of cadeucus. What a blessing today was! In thank you my creator TETRAGRAMMATION and My God ENKI and Goddess ISHTAR.

NEPTUNE THUNDERS Positions according to the Arcanum TAROT

The TAROT was created by METATRON Enoch based on the overall universal structure to be able to learn how it works. How to use it in accordance with our inner Solar system and our Astral Atman. I can truely say that I have manipulated the weather on 3 seperate occasions. Twice I've called and brought down Thunder and once record breaking Heat. With just spiritual basic Knowledge. No rituals but every time I was really into deep mental and spiritual life or death situations. In adn out of these higher realms and dimensions. You might need to read up on quite a few books to understand what I'm talking about.

If then you've done your diligence and have study'd then what I say should make sense. Back before the days of the Bear/Big Dipper it was draco. Draco was when the Gods walked the Earth. When my God ENKI created our race out of TIAMAT the great worm of the Abyss. ENKI instilled the TETRAGRAMMATION spark of light to our life. This light does not exist in the Abyss from which we were fashioned. Who are not dead but dreaming as they were defeated by my

God ENKI whose number is 40 a most excellent number and is my Father the Master Magician ruler of the Air. And his son MAROUK a General and Master of War. These are the Gods of the North from the Kingdom of ANU. The Gods left and charged the Watchers __ to look over us from which they've been doing ever since. The Watchers will Kill anything that trys to tresspass their assigned watch. This is the North of which the Archangel UR-REE-ALE is charged over. This kingdom of the NOrth of ANU can be what the Alaskan Pyramid and triange and UAP's sightings are all about. Why my Altar will Always face the North and why I must pay homage to my God and Father ENKI and my Goddess Mighty ISHTAR brightest of them all and Mistress to all the Gods who all have bowed ddown to. These are of the Living Gods.

So in accordance with the TAROT of the Angel META-TRON and the Alchemy of Kabbala the North is the direction we must face when performing a ritual to bring our given word from the Kingdom our crown of the West. The 1st 2nd &3rd Arcanum of the TAROT is what confirms this positioning. As we face North #1 is the Crown in the Kabbalistic tree in the TAROT it is the Magician with the Holy Eight and all his tools. #2 is another Sephorah to the Magicians left on the TAROT and this is the High Priestess our Kundalini Mother who gives Toirth to the word. Why She is on the West side where the Word comes from. The Kingdom of the West where the Archangel GA-BREE-EL is charged over. Whose star is Davids the six rayed double triange. #3 in the TAROT Arcanum then is the Empress with her seceptor of Authority with the whole world on it. She is on the Right side of the Magician which is also a perfect sync with the Kabbala and TAROT. It is on the East who the Archangel RA-FA-EL was given charge over.

RA-FA-ELS star is the Married Union of the double Pentagram also known as the star of our race. Where our Sun comes from. This Star is a true symbolic meaning. The Empress has her sceptor with the Earth on top and our Pentagram Union the ten rayed star belongs because We were given dominion over the Earth. To understand why this is the true star of the East you must know its Alchemical meanin. For all of us mena nd women from the West whove been indoctrinated by The adorable ones teachings and influenced byt he Bible etc. To achieve our God hood and Immortality and become masters of our inner star and Suns energy's fullest potential. It can only be done through sex. We must have a partner to achieve this greatness as only few have done. This Union is not meant to create a perfect child or life as were not supposed to spill our Ens Siminis. It is to truely activate our chakras and give the caduceus serpents the path to our crown and let the serpents wisom of the Angel METATRON and receive his 12 rayed crwon. Become like that of Enoch the Master. By empregnating our hearts and giving birth to a real existence outside of our known dimension. This is also why when facing North directly behind in the South is the Archangel MD-CHI-ALE whose crown star is the double unioned 2 rayed star of the West. The METATRON crown from the Kingdom of the South. All its wisdom and knowledge. I've said how to obtain this crown by explaining the first 3 Arcanums. Their are 21 Arcanums to pass starting with the fool. The wheel of fortune or also called the World. When learning the TAROT you'll find out that its very real when done right. My belief when practicing is when asking the World and Universe a question or for something we no doubt should face East as this is the direction of our Sun Star our world our life force and inner

TETRAGRAMMATRON energy. Then still facing East you should lay down so your head/crown is on the West in the direction of GA-BRE-EL where your answers/words shall be delivered by TETRAGRAMMATION for he is the Word. When in this posisiont of receiving were only at that position. Our High Prestess is in the North and the Empress is on our South. Once we get our word or answers we then perform the rituals of the North'nern Kingdom and speak to manifest this into our reality.

you might disagree but mind you Im practicing to achieve the Arcanum A.Z.f and all its secrets which takes true dedication and many years to learn. This is not Goetia, Asatru or druid etc. As they set up their religions all over the world to achieve their God Hoods. When Im saying from what I know and have learned in practice and experiences in and out of the circle. As Im coming from the West I believe our ultimate Pinnacle of Success thats been laid out for us to achieve is that of the Master Enoch and more that are not mentioned here. I put here what is to me the symbolism and Alchemical set up. The Bible does not teach this. To those whom this may bless unto thee the Kingdom and the Power and the Glory forever. May it be so!

If you have knowledge and will help me learn the Arcanum A.Z.f. or a beautiful blonde Petite Goddess willing to be my partner, or wanting to start a coven based on this Esoteric path contact me please. To start must be 40 years or younger unless already have many years of practice and knowledge to as where you understand everything. .

20 SHOTS..V..FEDERAL RESERVE .40 CAL

1. Blue Monday by various artist
2. G Style by Conejo
3. Next Level by Conejo
4. Red Alert by Conejo
5. Mob livin by Northern exposure
6. La Vida Es Dura by Conejo feat. Satiro/Bugzy 2 Guns
7. Raza Park by Jay Tee & Bably Bash
8. Fasten Your Seat Belts by Conejo
9. Venom Flow by Conejo
10. Wicked Games by The Weekend
11. El 24 by El Tigrillo Palma
12. El Bazucazo by El Tigrillo Palma
13. Music Blast by Conejo feat. Mr. Dee/Trouble kidd
14. Cold as Ice by Ava Max
15. Privat Number by Conejo
16. Yeyo by Conejo
17. In the Dark by Ava Max
18. Bossin Up by Mafia_2094
19. Ondata Di Criminalita by Conejo feat. Lil Pin/Prhome
20. Sleep Walker by Ava Max

www.ingramcontent.com/pod-product-compliance
Lightning Source LLC
Chambersburg PA
CBHW071914070526
44583CB00016B/1983